My sweetest hangover

Poetry - for the heart

A.V. Carter

My sweetest hangover

Published by Hidden Pond Media LLC

TABLE OF CONTENTS

*I wonder
*Matrix
*Too much
*Trouble
*Turn
*Yesterday remembered
*Like none before
*Dreams of you

"We love from a different place, and a different way.
And all I really know is I need you in my life.
And I never wanna do this without you,
'Cause we love"

Excerpt from the song "We Love"
By Ray Lavender (International R&B Singer and Actor)

13 seconds-

"13 Seconds"

The elevator door closes.

You touch my chin.

You hold my face with both your hands and pull my lips toward yours.

"9 Seconds"

My arms wrap around your shoulders and back.

You close your eyes.

Our lips part....Wow.

Our tongues touch...mmmm

Time stops.

"5 Seconds"

The world is no longer our background.

There are only night lights.

Our hearts beat....... together.

I suspect they always have.

"13 seconds" is the same as a lifetime with you!

I want lifetimes, **many** lifetimes with you.

A thought-

I thought about you yesterday.

And I walked into that thought.

I walked right into it as if it was a room.

I looked around and everything was in full bloom.

The fruit was ripe. The river was clear.

The birds sang and sang. I sat in the tall grass.

I lay back to rest. The wind was cool to arms.

I closed my eyes… you placed your hands on my cheeks.

I smiled. You place your lips on mine…

I shall never leave this place.

A wish-

I'm thinking,

I'm thinking,

I wish I was a wish.

If I was a wish, I would make everything alright for you.

I would let you wish to me.

I would become whatever you want, whatever you need.

Whatever you desire…

Hey wait, that's what I try to do now…

Oh, where was I, yeah,

I would create a world for you,

A world that would be a dream come true.

A dream that you could go to,

When you need to,

When you want to.

Hey wait, that's what I'm trying to do now…

Oh, where was I, yeah.

I…continue..

to…adore…

you.

I can't stop,

I won't stop.

It never ends,

In my mind, you are cinnamon to me.

Just….

Breath.

ADDICTED... BEFORE EVEN TRYING IT-

I find myself looking for reasons to be near you.

I find myself looking for ways to get you to be
near me.

It is good to see you.

It is intoxicating to be near you.

When I say intoxicating,

I mean there is a feeling of euphoria that
surrounds your very being.

In your presence I inhale it....constantly.

It is the air mixed with your essence, compounded
by your voice.

I am filled with wonder and delight by you.

Your stare traps me as sure as I am in a
cage....with you.

There is no lock on the door....yet, I will not leave.

You leave. I wait for you to return. I always will. I
always will. Because the times in between seeing
you...because the times in between hearing your
voice...does not count to me. I only count our
time together. And it is good for me.

To summon me, simply close your eyes...and say
my name.

Alive with you-

I am alive.

When I see you, I am alive.

When you say my name, I am alive.

When you touch my face with your hands,

I am alive.

Your love is overwhelming.

I am alive with it.

Your breath is life to me.

When I think about you,

My feelings can't explain…

When I'm not around you, my heart feels pain.

When I look at you, the memories of love flood my

every cell.

Like no one before, you cloud my mind.

I am not my own………I am ours.

I am alive with you.

ALL I SEE IS YOU-

I plan for my life to overlap yours.

Are you with me on this?

It will be difficult at times.

Our schedules will conflict.

Are you with me on this?

Don't fret.

My love for you knows no interruptions.

Are you with me on this?

Anger and depression will show their faces.

We must work through it.

Passion and joy is on the other side.

Are you with me on this?

Our bodies will change.

Our interest will evolve.

But, know this, I am here.

I am there, with you.

I am in, out, front, back,

Even under your feet to carry you.

We are one.

Are you with me on this?

When I close my eyes, all I see is you walking to me, across the landscape, that is, my mind.
I await you on the edge of forever.

I look at the clock. The second hand is not moving.
I smile. Time plays no role in our love.
Are you with me on this?

The sun and moon sit opposite each other in our sky.
Normal rules do not apply here.
When I close my eyes,….
All I see is you…

All through time-

I carefully position the last brick; my shift is
coming to an end.
My arms…ache.
The tower of Babel is near completion.
Chariots approach and the king is in the lead one.
Nimrod inspects and then even praises the work
being done.
A woman stands in the third chariot.
Our eyes meet.
Our love begins.

Hundreds of years pass….
Pharaoh now sits in his favorite lounge chair.
His sons run around him laughing and playing.
This time I am standing with his other counselors.
Processions of slaves are passing by.
You trip in front of me.
As you look up, our eyes meet.
Our love begins again….

Time moves on…
Now I find myself bowing before Solomon.
Terrified, I am!
It is now common knowledge of my affair with his
youngest daughter.

Standing before him, you plead my case....to no avail.

I am sentenced to death.

Our love is interrupted.

Time moves on....

The Roman Empire.

I go to deliver a letter for my master.

I am nearly run over in the street by a horse rider!

As I stand up, our eyes meet.

The fire still burns strong between us.....

My king has sent me to kill count Brasco and his entire family for treason.

Upon entering the courtyard, I give the order to my men.

The massacre begins.

Knife in hand, I grab Brasco's wife, turning her to face me.

Wow, it is you.

I put my blade away.

Over and over, place and time has no bearing on our love.

It goes on...

And....and...

As I look into your eyes,

I remember you as Isabel.

Watching your peasants work the fields from a
window in your castle.
I am one of the moors, now.
And soon, we will take Spain from your people.
I remember you as rebeka,
one of the first children born in the "new world".
Pilgrims, you were called then.
You got lost in the woods and found me....
They never saw you, again.

It is not in the names,
It is to be with you.

I remember you stepping off of the slave ship.
Nebala, you were called then.
You had the look of a proud princess in shackles,
along with fear on your face.
I stand midway in the auction crowd.
And I am ready to mortgage my entire plantation
to have you.
Our eyes meet...
You begin to smile as you are flooded with
memories of our past lives.
You know then, that you are safe.
Whenever you appear, wherever you appear, I
am already there waiting for you.
Our love....continues.

Ambrosia-

Cloudy days and nights without stars

Until you came into my life.

Clear skies now greet me.

My nights are illuminated now

As I think and long for you,

Every minute of the day.

I just want to let you know

that with the love I'm free.

I can feel because of the love.

I can smile because of the love.

The love is an ambrosia that is all I Need.

The ambrosia……….is…..you.

Do not adjust your T.V.-

This is as real as can be.

You can feel it in your heart

You can smell it from afar

You can believe we're not apart

Do not adjust your T.V.

The line is seen by none

The line is growing stronger

The line is felt by one

The line is like a hunger

Do not adjust your T.V.

The distance becomes smaller

The space becomes closer.

The closeness of a caller

The thing grows never smaller

Do not adjust your T.V.

It has become a thing of its own

Do not adjust your T.V.

Because it tells the truth.

I am with you.

Eternity-

I've gone from here to eternity.

It was not as far as far as I believed it to be.

It did not take as long as I thought it would.

I've gone from here to eternity.

All I needed was the right guide.

To show me the way, you are that guide.

It was as far as the farthest star.

But, as close as your touch.

As far as a goal.

As close as your smile.

As far as the end of time.

As close as our minds in sync.

It's bright here.

But, there is no sun.

It is cool here and warm at the same time.

It's soothing, caring, and safe here.

It's how I feel when I'm holding you in my arms.

Or, looking in your eyes,

Or caressing your skin,

Or watching you walk,

Or, inhaling your intoxicating scent.

It is you.

Every day-

You have never left my side since the day we met.

"How?" you say?

From that day forward, you have been in my head.

I drive in my car and I hear you singing to me.

(The radio is not turned on.)

I go jogging and birds bring me messages from you.

I go swimming and I see you at each end of my lane.

From that first day, you have been in my head.

I lay down and in the split second between awake and sleep…you say, "Goodnight." to me.

If my mind was real estate, then, you would own a large portion of it.

And, you do.

From the day we met, you have occupied my free time.

I hold your hand.

I squeeze you in my arms.

I brush my lips to yours.

Because, from the day we met, you have never left my side….

In my mind.

Forever draws near-

When you walk in the room
There, is no need for light.
As you enter, the air changes,
Then, you smile and everything is bright.
The wall melt away and forever draws near.
You speak without talking, I can hear you oh so
clear.
I move to you, you move to me.
When the wall melt away, and forever draws near.
As you put your arms around me, our bodies
merge.
Our hearts become one; it's like an electric surge.
For two to become one? Is that why were here?
When the wall melt away, and forever draws near.
I look down at our bodies, they stand ever so still.
The breeze takes us up to where it will.
In my ear I hear you say,
"There is no tomorrow, there is only....today."
When forever draws near and the walls melt
away.

Fork in the road-

Either, I am slow, or you are great at hiding my feelings.

I think you want me.

I need more than a smile.

Am I the only one felling like this?

You seem to not want to test the waters "thinking" it might be deep.

I won't let you drown.

I know how to swim.

You say that you have always been mine.

Show me then.

I need more than a smile.

I won't be okay until I have you for myself.

If I cannot have you when I want to,

I will settle for when I can.

I am standing at the crossroad.

Meet me on the left and I move closer to you.

Point me to the right and I fade away.

Choose…..today.

My feelings will not change…

Believe this,

"I have loved you from the day we met.

And I will love you long, long after I put this pen down."

Say, "I want you, too."

Your eyes say it quite often.

I need you to tell me with your voice.

Tell me.

Here I am-

The elders said that we did not ask to come here.
But, here I am.
They said that, for a time, we were not allowed to
be fathers.
To father, yes but, not be a father.
Sadly, we learned well.
And, here I am.

There were places we could not live.
Things we could not own.
Jobs we could not do.
Education, for a time, was not an option.
I learned well.
And here I am.

I was told I could not achieve.
I was told, I was…different.
But, the elders passed a message along
from generation to generation.
From father to daughter, mother to son, father to
daughter, and mother to me.
That message was always the same.

You can achieve.
You can learn.

You must be a father.

You can have that job.

You can live there.

You…can…achieve.

I believed it, and I learned well.

Now, I am a father.

You are my wife.

I make that money.

The elders were right!

Because, here I am.

I'm there-

Just something to let you know I'm there.

Reach for me, I'm there.

Listen to me breathe,

I'm there.

Feel my tongue, I'm there.

The heat emanating from my body, I'm there.

The heat emanating from your body, I'm there.

From…our bodies, we are there.

YES!

It must be you-

The sun feels so good.

The day is better.

The clouds appear to smile at me.

It must be you.

The flowers are all in bloom.

The air feels like when you caress my skin.

It must be you.

The people I see, I really don't see.

They talk to me, but I only hear your voice.

It must be you.

I suspect you were meant to be my lady.

It may never be.

But, that does not make it untrue.

It must be you.

You got me. Mind, body, and soul….

I anticipate our next rendezvous.

It must be you.

It is you.

You.

Love you-

Ifeel it was fate. I

Looked into the glass.

On the other side was us.

Vibrant and intense.

Every day better than the last.

Your love more than enough.

Our love something growing immensely.

Under your sky, I am home.

More than enough-

With high anticipation I come to the place where I hope you will be.

To see you is more than enough…

I hear you before I see you and I can't contain my smile.

My hands tingle, my breathing slows down.

Woman, you bring calm to me.

To see you is more than enough…

I walk toward the sound of your voice.

There you are…pause…breath.

Pause, breath…

Our eyes connect.

Wow.

The invisible hooks are lodged as deep as ever.

Intense? Yes. Pain? No.

To see you is more than enough…

My day is complete at this point.

No matter what the time of day it is.

After seeing you, after being with you, it is all good.

To see you is more than enough…

My beautiful distraction-

As you glide across the room

I lose focus and refocus on your hips.

All the way until you leave the room.

And then, I follow you out of the room.

I will miss my T.V. show…again.

We are about to leave for work.

You lean over to kiss me.

Your saliva is an opiate to me.

I lose focus on the current objective.

We will be late for work …again.

I am constantly, pleasantly distracted by you, and

I love it.

May the distractions never cease in our lives.

As you walk towards me it feels like Christmas

Eve.

Your touch is like the fourth of July.

Your presence near me is intoxicating.

I struggle to stay sober.

I lose.

The wanting for you never subsides.

I want you even more when you're not around.

Sunset,. With a Cigar in my left hand, a glass of

Scotch in my right, I sit waiting for you.

Just thinking of you is like the cool of the evening.

My life continues when you take your place
beside me.
Nothing comes before you, everything comes
after you……..

No answers-

I have been trying to figure out why I am pulled toward you.

No luck.

I am pulled toward you from the inside.

How are you doing this?

Stop.

Alas, no luck.

The more I am around you the stronger the pull.

The more I am away from you, well, the pull is even stronger.

Stop pulling me.

But, you never do.

A thought.

Is it you pulling me or is it me meeting you hallway?

I stare too much at you.

Your eyes sparkle when you look at me.

Did you know that?

Or, am I just seeing what I hope to see?

I need to stop.

No luck.

I want to say things like we, us, and ours.

Will it ever be like that?

Do you feel it?

If you don't, then, it never was there.

One moment-

I am always on the go.

I got to get this money for us.

But, one moment is more than enough.

I can't take you to dinner every night.

But, sharing a moment is a lifetime to me.

We can't always go walking.

I got to get this money for us.

I can and will let you know, that I do cherish you.

I can give my undivided attention when I am near.

I can hold you in my arms.

You can cry on my shoulders.

Know,…that my feeling are unwavering,

unchanging and unconditional.

I can't have you forever,

But, forever you have me.

Signed by you-

Your name is all over me.

Can you not see it?

You are the diamond perched on the edge of the sand.

I spend hours adoring you.

What we have stands outside of time.

This has been before.

This is now.

This is tomorrow.

This has always and will always…be.

It is you that makes it so.

Singing-

I bend the very fabric of time

to bring you close to me.

Come.

I love you in and outside of time.

Listen.

The music is for your heart.

Listen to it.

I sing for you.

Speed-

Heart racing,

I just stare.

Patient, yes.

I just stare.

I am lost in your eyes.

I…..just………stare.

Lips touching……

heart racing.

Speed.

Sunset-

The snow has just started to fall.

It will be very cold tonight.

I stand looking across the water, thinking of you.

The long leather coat keeps me warm until you

come to take its place.

Life slowly goes on…

Then, I see your face, again.

I hold you in my arms, again.

Time stops when you are in my arms, again.

Everything comes after….you.

Talk to me-

You bend the very sunlight to your will.

You have your own star and it follows you across the stage of life.

It compliments your beauty.

The flowers want to be near you,

You compliment then with your splendor.

The wind carriers your voice…

It allows others the privilege of hearing….

the sweet song that you call…talk.

The wind even caters to you.

Your aura is intoxicating.

Your eyes are the window to a passion that must be unleashed in measured doses.

Or I fear the recipient being overwhelmed, with its intensity.

I am humbled to be in your presence.

You increase my essence.

It is right to love you…

The way I do-

For most, the easy way is to put you on a
pedestal.

Too easy.

Many would lavish you with physical treasures.

Too easy…

Even easier is to take you to exotic places around
the world.

Dazzle you?

Too easy.

And then…I…know.

I want to feel your breath on my skin.

Blow in my ear.

Yes.

I know that I would count each second in your
presence as amazing…

Many would buy you a mansion. You deserve it.

Too easy...

I would sit in the park with, lay your head in my
lap and listen to you tell me of your dreams.

I would paddle us across the lake to picnic on the
far side.

All our days would be similar to a lazy summer
evening.

I would walk with you.

I would whisper to you.

I would hold your hand.

I would listen to you.

I would want you.

I think I always have.

I must exercise control.

Lest, I be lost in your smile,

Yet, again.

I WONDER-

I wonder what is going on behind your eyes.
I wonder, because your eyes burn clear and
bright.
Are you thinking of me?
If eyes are the windows to the soul, then it must
be wonderful to be intimate with you.
Sometimes, when you smile, your soul spills out
and I am in bewilderment because you…glow.
Are you thinking of me?

Yesterday, you were walking toward me and it
was like the morning sun brightening and
warming the new day.
Being near you is the absence of winter, the
absence of pain, the presence of joy, the
presence of warmth, and the presence of peace.
Are you thinking of me?

As you awake each day,
Work each hour,
Relax in the evening,
As you lay in bed,
Are you thinking of me?

I think of you.

Even now…and I walk into that thought.

I walk right into it as if it was a room.

I look around and everything is in full bloom.

The fruit is ripe.

The river runs clear.

The birds sing and sing.

I sit in the tall grass.

I lay back to rest.

The wind is cool to my arms.

I close my eyes, you place your hands on my cheeks.

I smile. You place your lips on mine.

I shall never leave this place.

Matrix-

You make me re-think, re-evaluate,
how I measure time.
Einstein's theory is thrown upside down when you
are involved.
Who are you?

You come near me and the clocks stop.
The sun stands still for us. Time obeys you.
You walk away from me and the
world.....continues.
Who are you?

I do not age when, I am with you. The years fall
away from my body.
Your essence is pure rejuvenation.
Who are you?

I suspect that a lifetime could be spent with
you…in one afternoon.
Dare we try?
Who are you?
Just for me.
Unconditional.
Either you are the one for me
or I am caught in some kind of Matrix.

TOO MUCH-

I see you and I smile on the inside. It is hot.

It is not quite heat, but, more like a warm shower.

You engulf me without trying. I like that….. a lot.

You speak and it is a song that I know…. Sing to me.

Your smile……I look forward to it. Too much.

Your walk….

Your conversation….I want to listen to you all night.

I want to be around you…..too much.

I squeeze every drop of every second that I am with you.

And later … I replay it in my mind ….. slowly.

Oh… for you to match this feeling.

Tell me you….. do.

Still…I do.

Too much.

Trouble-

You know you're in trouble,

When you think and smile,

Because, she will be back in a while

You know you're in trouble.

When her words matter alot

When her walk is neat…to watch.

You know you're in trouble,

When she brightens your day

When around her, longer, you would stay.

You know you're in trouble,

When you spend time in your mind, in that

alternate place with her sipping wine

You know you're in trouble,

So, open your eyes and realize

That reality is not fantasy,

And you wonder…"Will she ever be mine?"

Turn-

Turn around….
I need to see your face.
It is the morning sun that warms the world.
Turn around….

So, I can share my smile with you.
I adore you being apart of my day.
Turn around….

I want to gather the items that touch your skin.
Those items become special under your touch.
Turn around….

Walk with me, hold my hand, and let me kiss you.
Tell me if you can….
Turn around…
And love me. Love you. Love us…just…
turn around.

Yesterday remembered-

There was a time……..
I cleaned that knife….daily.
Another life
My sandals were the softest leather.
I wore a head-wrap to keep the sweat out of my
eyes.
And a sheep skin cloak to protect my skin from
the sun.
A rectangle shaped shield.
My stamina was…….forever.
As I sit under an old oak tree, the call starts.
Softly and then it gradually grows into a constant
wave.
I remember…Even now …
I remember.
I hear your call from deep inside of me.
It resonates like a bell inside my head.
So, out of the jungle I walk…and into the desert I
go.
The sand is so hot.
Days later, I walk out of the sand and onto the
beach.
The shoreline is breathtaking. I walk to the small
empty boat.
There is a necklace inside. I know it well.

It's the necklace I made for you when we were wed.

A sigh escapes from my lips.

For three days I sit by the water's edge.

"You know you cannot swim." I said aloud, over and over again.

But, her voice is strong within me. There is an unbreakable cord that connects us and it pulls hard on my heart.

Finally I stand.

I push the boat into the water and jump in…

And far away … You smile.

"Does he still have the sheep skin I gave him?" she wonders. "Does he even remember me?"

When she closes her eyes she can see me.

See me moving toward her.

Step by step, out of the jungle, through the desert and onto the water.

Her man…will only rest during the heat of the day.

It is so hot during the day.

It was just 3 nights before that she stood on the edge of the sands and called to him from deep within her heart.

Even now, with her eyes closed, she says to herself, "I know he felt me. I know it. He is coming for me. He said he would. I believe in him. We are ...one."

The distance between them is not her reality.

Yet, she is still on a boat sailing north.

She barely had time to leave something for him in the boat that they did not take.

She was beaten for being the last to board the boat.

It is not good to be the last one...These people don't play...Slavery is fast approaching. Cold and hungry she whispers to herself,

"I must believe that he is coming".....

And she was right ...

Like none before-

It was your grandmother, that first said,

Eventually I would come..

Exactly, when you need him..

Yes, that one.

Different from the others;

She knew that I would be.

To the young ones without a father,...

a teacher I will be.

Responsibility sits heavy on my shoulders.

I am comfortable with its weight.

Flawed, I am.

Mistakes, yes, those I will make,

But Broken, I am not.

I will not let you down.

Nor, shatter your dreams.

For, they are mine, too.

Let me fill in the seams,

Mine is to influence and help all.

To inspire others, just like me,

Role model, I will be called.

Just close your eyes and it's me.

I got your back,

Lean on me,

On my shoulders place your brow,

I will never give up on you.

I don't know how.

Like none you've met before.

Dreams of you-

I find myself standing here
remembering all the years that
we have spent together. Yet, I
know that they never
happened…yet.

ABOUT THE AUTHOR

A.V. Carter is a husband, father and Motivational Speaker. When asked what he is most proud of his answer was husband and serving in the military during Desert Storm. "I joined the Military in 1990 and to my shock (I know, I know...I DID join an Army) we went to war! During this period, I realized how important relationships were. I realized how important it is to let that person know how you feel. They cannot read your mind so you need to say it in some way. I am married to a woman that believes in me even when I don't believe in me. This work was inspired by her on so many levels. This work began during that time. In my opinion, there is nothing greater than to have someone believe in you."

Made in the USA
Lexington, KY
06 June 2017